AF422468

be bold.

dymeata b.

DEDICATION

This book is dedicated to every person who struggles with self-sabotage. I pray that you find the strength to break free from the chains that hold you back. This book is a testament to your resilience and a reminder that you are not alone on this journey. I pray that God centers you around people who have your answer and not your problem. I hope that this book empowers you to unlearn who you were so that you can become the person He called you to be. Embrace your journey towards self-discovery.

TABLE OF CONTENTS

INTRODUCTION

I want to remind you today of who you truly are in Christ. Too often, we allow the world and the enemy to shape our identity, causing us to feel inadequate, unworthy, and unable to fulfill the great plans God has for our lives.

But the Word of God declares that before the foundation of the world, you were chosen and destined for greatness in Him (Ephesians 1:4). You were not an afterthought or a mistake - you were intricately designed by the Master Creator with a divine purpose.

Like Gideon, you may feel small, insignificant, and ill-equipped for the task ahead. But God sees you differently. He calls you a "mighty man of valor" (Judges 6:12), one who is anointed and empowered to overcome every obstacle and defeat every enemy that stands in your way.

The enemy would love nothing more than to keep you stuck in a mindset of inadequacy, convincing you that you can never rise above your current circumstances. But I declare to you today - that is a lie from the pit of hell! You are a child of the Most High God, a co-heir with Christ, destined for victory.

It's time to stop hiding your gifts and talents, stop doubting your abilities, and start walking in the fullness of who God has called you to be. The world is waiting for you to rise up and fulfill your divine purpose. Your family, your community, your nation - they are all depending on you to step into the champion that you were created to be.

So, I encourage you, to fix your eyes on the eternal, not the temporal. Refuse to be defined by your past or your present struggles. Instead, see yourself through the lens of God's perfect design. You are chosen. You are anointed. You are mighty.

The battle may be fierce, but the victory is already yours. Go forth in the power of the Holy Spirit and watch as God uses you to transform your world. This is your time. This is your season. This is your moment to shine.

As you read through the book, my prayer is that the Lord strengthen you, empower you, and propel you into the destiny He has prepared for you. I decree that the spirit of self-sabotage is broken over you and your bloodline TODAY! It's time to become ALL that God has called you to be, do ALL that He has equipped you to do, and possess ALL that He promised to you.

CLASS IS NOW IN SESSION.

CHAPTER ONE

UNDERSTANDING SELF-SABOTAGE

I do not understand what I do. For what I want to do I do not do, but what I hate I do. Romans 7:15

Have you ever found yourself doing certain things that you know very well are hurting your life but cannot seem to stop? Let me be the first to admit that I have, and at some point, it took me getting sick and tired of holding myself back. I refer to such things in this book as self-sabotaging habits. The act of sabotage refers to destroying or undermining something, usually stealthily. The word is most frequently used in spying or commercial scenarios where an insider is causing damage since it usually implies direct and purposeful engagement on the part of the saboteur. When this harmful activity is aimed at oneself, it is called self-sabotage. You might not even be aware that you're doing it at first. However, negative habits might be regarded as a type of psychological self-harm when they persistently undercut your attempts. Self-sabotage can take many various forms, in our lives. However, there are a few typical, recurrent instances.

For example, let's say that you "forgot" a deadline or didn't fully prepare a presentation. You may arrive late to work every day. You might frequently put off tasks that you know you should accomplish, yet you continue to procrastinate to get the things done. You start tasks but never complete them. Even when God presents an opportunity of an open door, you feel unprepared to walk through it. Or maybe, you have a genius entrepreneurial idea something you want to accomplish but you can never seem to get started. When you attempt to accomplish your goals and suddenly stop for no apparent reason, it's another obvious indicator that you are engaging in self-sabotage. You have the ability and desire to succeed, yet something keeps you stuck. UGH!

Now let's pause for a second and talk about negative self-talk. I am grateful to God for choosing me as His vessel to encourage and empower women. It's what I was born to do. But don't get it twisted, I have had numerous encounters battling with negative self-talk. Leading up to and during the pandemic, I found myself trapped in a deep well of depression. The weight of hopelessness and uncertainty overwhelmed me, fueled by various factors. One of the main contributors was the overwhelming sense of loneliness as I had unanswered questions about our youngest daughter, Malaya-Skye's development delays. New to a big city where we had no connections besides my mom. The isolation grew unbearable, casting a dark shadow over my days. As the negativity consumed me, secretly crying "why me?", and constantly voicing my insecurities to my husband about feeling stuck and not worthy of success. Now don't leave me out here by myself, I'm sure you have had moments in which you told yourself you're inadequate or undeserving of achievement. This behavior is the root cause of self-sabotage. You start having thoughts along the lines of "You can't do that!" "You don't deserve that." "If you try, you'll probably just fail anyway. "You don't have enough money or experience." We may have all seen actions similar to these at some point. However, some of us are more likely than others to self-sabotage, and it can be challenging to acknowledge when we're acting in this way. We must pay close attention to the warning signs and not dismiss them.

In our journey of self-discovery, we often will encounter unbearable obstacles, some of which are things we caused ourselves. Self-sabotage is a perplexing phenomenon in which we knowingly or unknowingly hold up our own progress, dreams, and well-being. I like to call this a "You Problem". Self-sabotage manifests in various forms, ranging from procrastination and self-doubt to destructive habits and behaviors. At its essence, self-sabotage is a coping mechanism that is rooted in fear and self-preservation.

I know what it feels like to have worked toward a vital goal only to have it all fall apart because of poor choices. As I write at this moment to complete my goal of completing this book in hopes that it will empower women, I have experienced tension and anxiety while attempting to accomplish this huge goal. If I give up now, I may become increasingly disappointed, disheartened, and upset with myself. If I give up now, I could possibly become stuck by these emotions and unable to complete this book. All of these indicate self-sabotage. Self-sabotage can also damage our connections with other people and erodes our sense of confidence and self-worth. With each setback that we experience, we "prove" to ourselves that we are incapable of doing the thing we want to do. Apostle says ***I do not understand what I do. For what I want to do, I do not do, but what I hate, I do***. Romans 7:15

That's the simple definition of some of us putting ourselves into sabotage. Whatever self-sabotaging behaviors you have, it's essential that you overcome them if you are going to make the most of your life, business or career. Individuals engage in behaviors that sabotage their efforts, creating a self-fulfilling prophecy that reinforces their negative beliefs and fears.

Jonah, a prophet called by God to deliver a message to the people of Nineveh, initially resisted his divine assignment out of fear and reluctance. He feared the repercussions and perhaps doubted his abilities, Jonah attempts to flee from God's command, boarding a ship bound for Tarshish. However, his attempts to escape are interrupted by a fierce storm sent by God, eventually leading to his being swallowed by a great fish.

Jonah's story is the essence of self-sabotage – the fear-driven resistance to fulfilling one's purpose and what God called him to do. Despite being chosen by God for a sacred assignment, Jonah allows his fears and doubts to dictate his actions, ultimately leading to his downfall. Yet, even in despair, Jonah finds redemption through surrender and obedience to God's will, illustrating the transformative power of divine grace.

One common manifestation of self-sabotage is the fear of failure. I can admit that almost every dream, vision and assignment God has given me, I have strongly felt the fear of failure trying to creep up on me. Despite harboring aspirations and dreams, I have sabotaged my efforts out of fear of falling short or failing to meet the expectations of others. This fear often stems from past experiences of failure or criticism, leading to a debilitating cycle of avoidance and self-sabotage. Similarly, the fear of success can drive self-sabotaging behaviors as individuals grapple with feelings of unworthiness or impostor syndrome. Sabotage has been a common theme throughout history and stories. One example is Joseph's Story in the Bible. This Story shows how betrayal, envy, resilience, and redemption play out. It shows us how sabotage isn't just something that happens externally; sometimes, it can come from people close to us, as seen in Joseph's Story.

Joseph, the eleventh son of Jacob, was favored by his father, who gifted him a coat of many colors, symbolizing his unique status among his siblings. This act of favoritism ignited jealousy and resentment among Joseph's brothers, leading them to plot his downfall. Their envy manifested into a deliberate act of sabotage when they seized the opportunity to sell Joseph into slavery, deceiving their father into believing that a wild animal had killed him. The betrayal Joseph experienced from his flesh and blood illustrates how internal sabotage can arise from familial dynamics, envy, and the desire for power or recognition. His brothers' actions were driven by a toxic combination of jealousy and a sense of inadequacy, leading them to resort to drastic measures to eliminate their perceived threat.

Joseph's journey into slavery in Egypt marked the beginning of a series of trials and tribulations, where he faced further acts of sabotage orchestrated by others. Despite being falsely accused of misconduct and thrown into prison, Joseph's resilience and unwavering faith enabled him to rise above his circumstances. His ability to interpret dreams caught the attention of Pharaoh, ultimately leading to his appointment as the second-in-command in Egypt. His Story also reflects how internal sabotage can manifest from within oneself. During his rise to power, Joseph had the opportunity to seek revenge on his brothers when they came to Egypt seeking food during a famine. Instead of succumbing to the temptation of retaliation, Joseph chose forgiveness and reconciliation, exemplifying the triumph of virtue over vindictiveness. Beloved makes a choice to be set free from the bondage of sabotage.

Why We Do Self-Sabotage?

We, including me, all engage in sabotage and self-destructive habits for a variety of reasons. It's possible that we picked up self-sabotaging habits and behaviors as kids. You may be a person who was raised in an abusive home where they were always on guard can develop into a guarded, confrontational adult who finds it difficult to maintain peaceful relationships even though they are aware of the harm their actions might cause.

Some people turn to self-destructive habits, such as drug or alcohol abuse, as a coping mechanism for emotional distress or traumatic experiences from the past. Furthermore, some people can discover that their negative thoughts, habits, and low self-esteem have become deeply established in their attitudes, behaviors, and perceptions. Individuals who self-sabotage may have developed biases or a negative outlook on life. Due to past traumas and deeply rooted self-destructive behaviors, their perspective on the world may be more pessimistic or scared. They might have started to think that life would always be too hard, that they'll never be able to find love, or that they'll never be able to achieve that promotion.

This thinking frequently prevents people from developing, changing, and going through good shifts.

Low self-esteem is one of the leading causes of self-sabotage. The roots of this can vary greatly, but the outcomes are always the same: feelings of inadequacy or worthlessness, the conviction that you are undeserving of achievement, and even self-loathing. If you succeed, you might be concerned that your coworkers will be envious, or your family will think less of you if you fail. Negative self-talk stemming from these ingrained attitudes and emotions feeds your anxieties and self-destructive tendencies.

Some people self-sabotage because it makes them feel in control of their situations. By sabotaging and rescuing a problem, they might receive a short-term boost to their self-confidence. It may even feel temporarily thrilling. However, these "rewards" are destructive in the long term. Sabotage is a destructive act that undermines, impedes, or disrupts the functioning or success of a person, group, organization, or system. It often arises from anger, envy, greed, or a desire for revenge, leading individuals to resort to underhanded tactics to achieve their goals or gratify their desires at the expense of others. While sabotage may seem like a modern phenomenon driven by personal or political motives, its roots can be traced back to biblical times, where we find examples of characters who engaged in acts of sabotage for various reasons. One such character is Delilah, whose betrayal of Samson by cutting off his hair – the secret to his strength – resulted in his capture and downfall (Judges 16:4-21). Delilah's sabotage was fueled by greed, as the Philistine rulers promised her a large sum of money in exchange for discovering the source of Samson's power. Her betrayal not only led to Samson's physical captivity but also to the loss of his purpose and position as a leader chosen by God.

Sabotage has been around for a long time. It means purposely ruining or messing with someone else's plans or efforts. People do this for many reasons, such as jealousy, anger, fear, or insecurity. Looking at why people sabotage others using stories from the Bible can help us understand why people behave this way. Envy is a big reason people sabotage others. Let's visit the Story of Cain and Abel from the Book of Genesis. Cain was jealous of his brother Abel because God liked Abel's gift more. This jealousy leads Cain to kill Abel, showing how envy can cause people to do terrible things without realizing the consequences. This Story warns us about how destructive envy can be and how it can drive people to extreme actions to protect their success or status.

What about King Saul's jealousy towards David? Saul's fear of David's growing popularity and recognition as a brave warrior led him to repeatedly attempt to kill David out of envy and insecurity (1 Samuel 18:6-11). Saul's actions can be interpreted as sabotage, as he sought to undermine David's reputation, influence, and, ultimately, his life to preserve his power and position as king.

The story of Joseph and his brothers in Genesis is a classic example of familial sabotage rooted in envy and rivalry. Joseph's brothers, consumed by jealousy over their father's favoritism towards him, conspired to sell him into slavery and deceive their father into believing that Joseph had been killed by a wild animal (Genesis 37:12-36). Their sabotage not only shattered their family unity but also set in motion a chain of events that ultimately led to Joseph's rise to power in Egypt and the eventual reconciliation of the family. That's called FAVOR. But that's for another book. Sabotage illuminates the destructive nature of such actions and their motivations. Whether driven by greed, envy, fear, or a thirst for power, sabotage often stems from sinful inclinations that seek to elevate oneself at the expense of others, disregarding the principles of love, justice, and integrity upheld in the Bible.

CHAPTER TWO

THE IMPACT OF SELF-SABOTAGE ON OUR LIVES

The desire of the lazy man kills him, for his hands refuse to labor. He covets greedily all day, But the righteous gives and does not spare.
Proverbs 21:25-26.

I hope, that so far you have acknowledged your sabotaging behaviors, whether it was from you to yourself or towards someone else. Most people have engaged in self-sabotaging behavior at some point in life. However, when self-defeating habits and behaviors become ingrained, this can negatively impact our mental health, self-esteem, and self-confidence. Have you noticed how often you set goals and dream about something, and before you know it, life throws you a distraction, you find yourself procrastinating and putting things off and of course, nothing happens? Distractions, such as the unending notifications and text messages from our phones from the kids who text you about going out with friends or if they can have the last of the ice cream. Or maybe the conversations and memes of social media scrolling, or even the time we waste watching television, all act as potent catalysts for our procrastination. They divert our attention from the task at hand, luring us into a never-ending loop of temporary gratification. With each distraction, our focus fades, and our commitment to completing our responsibilities diminishes. Time slips away as we succumb to the temptation of indulging in things that don't serve us, leaving the important things like the assignments from God neglected. The more we allow distractions to infiltrate our lives, the deeper we sink into the quicksand of procrastination, struggling to regain our lost time and regain control of our priorities. It's like an invisible force is preventing you from achieving your desired goals. You experience internal resistance, subconsciously blocking realizing your plans and aspirations. This phenomenon is known as self-sabotage.

Self-sabotage is a subtle and sophisticated enemy penetrating all areas of your life. It spoils relationships, ruins careers, and jeopardizes your health. But why does it happen? Why do we become our greatest adversaries on the road to happiness and success? I suggest reading a few situations involving it to understand better self-sabotaging, which may be helpful.

Procrastination can be a typical example of self-sabotaging. While procrastinating occasionally can be understandable, it's when we make it a habit to put things off until the last minute that can be harmful and you become stuck.

For example, let's say you have a presentation tomorrow, you know you'll do better if you research and practice. But in the back of your mind, you start to feel that you're not good enough or won't do well so you put less effort into preparing. Then, once it's time for your moment, you need more preparation, and your anxiety and stress rises. Now you're frustrated and feeling defeated. However, repeated self-sabotaging behavior can be more painful if similar situations happen frequently. Self-sabotaging or self-destructive behavior can occur in all areas of life, including school, work, social life, and relationships.

Another common way we self-sabotage is through our love and dating relationships. I know someone right now who had love, but they didn't feel lovable, nor did they see love looking at them right in the face because they were blinded by past hurt. Some of you reading this may have sabotage by avoiding dating altogether, affirming the inner belief that love isn't out there for you. But they didn't feel lovable, nor did they see love looking at them right in the face. Some of you reading this may have self-sabotage by avoiding dating altogether, affirming the inner belief that love isn't out there for you. Alternatively, you act destructively in relationships by cheating or being emotionally unavailable to your partner. Sis, let me reaffirm you today, love is looking for you. One bad relationship doesn't end love. People who self-sabotage don't want to be unhappy. Some people may not realize their destructive behavior and that they're standing in their own way.

When we self-sabotage, we can feel that we cannot reach the goals we've set. Feeling like we can't achieve any of our goals or life dreams can be immensely demoralizing and can have a significantly negative impact on our mental health. When we self-sabotage, it may feel like we're saving ourselves from the pain of potential failure. Instead, it can put us in a cycle of negative emotions about ourselves, leading to negative consequences that appear to affirm those beliefs. In the professional sphere, self-sabotage is expressed by postponing projects and deadlines. A person consciously avoids career advancement due to fear of responsibility or lacking confidence in their abilities.

In business, self-sabotage manifests in an unwillingness to expand a company, attract new clients, or take reasonable risks for fear of failure. Limiting beliefs such as "I'm not fit for this" sabotages our advancement. If you have been following me over the years, I have launched businesses and many products. They all started out as an idea. There were nights that I could barely sleep from the excitement of planning the vision that God had given me. But then when it was close to launching, I would freeze up by fear and the thoughts of not "feeling" good enough. Not being a certain size, or maybe not having the right aesthetics for content. And I would remain in neutral. By the way, I'm still in therapy for that to hold myself accountable.

In personal relationships, self-sabotage is often related to the fear of emotional intimacy and openness to a partner. A person unconsciously distances himself, provokes conflicts, or builds protective barriers based on experience. This prevents trusting a partner and building harmonious relationships. According to an adverse scenario, self-sabotage manifests in repeated mistakes when choosing a partner.

Self-sabotage in health is most clearly expressed in the form of bad habits: overeating, smoking, alcohol abuse, etc. A person ignores the body's signals and neglects a healthy lifestyle. Self-sabotaging behavior also manifests in the unwillingness to exercise, sleep, and diet. Fear of change prevents changing the destructive scenario.

Understanding the forms of self-sabotage and their consequences helps recognize destructive patterns and begin to overcome them.

The impact of self-sabotage can be far-reaching, affecting various areas of our lives, including relationships, careers, and personal fulfillment. In relationships, for example, self-sabotage may manifest as fear of intimacy or vulnerability, leading us to push away potential partners or sabotage healthy connections. In our careers, self-sabotage can prevent us from pursuing our passions, taking on new challenges, or advancing in our chosen field. Self-sabotage can also have profound effects on our mental and emotional well-being, contributing to stress, anxiety, and feelings of inadequacy. When we constantly undermine our efforts or berate ourselves for perceived failures, we erode our self-esteem and confidence, creating a vicious cycle of negativity and self-doubt. Over time, this can lead to depression, burnout, and a sense of hopelessness about our prospects.

Self-sabotage is an expected behavior that can profoundly impact our lives. It refers to the destructive patterns of thought and behavior we engage in, often unconsciously, hindering our progress and success. In the Bible, many characters' stories illustrate the consequences of self-sabotage and provide valuable lessons for us to learn from. Let's explore some of these characters and how their experiences can shed light on the impact of self-sabotage on our lives.

One of the Bible's most well-known examples of self-sabotage is the story of Adam and Eve in the Book of Genesis. Adam and Eve were living in the Garden of Eden, enjoying a perfect relationship with God and each other. However, when they disobeyed God's command not to eat from the tree of the knowledge of good and evil, they set off a chain of events that led to their expulsion from the garden. Their decision to ignore God's instructions was a form of self-sabotage that had far-reaching consequences not only for themselves but for all of humanity.

Another biblical character who exemplifies the impact of self-sabotage is King Saul. God chose Saul to be the first king of Israel, but his insecurity and jealousy led him to make decisions that ultimately cost him his throne. Instead of trusting in God's plan and seeking His guidance, Saul gave in to his fears and insecurities, leading him to self-destruction. His story is a cautionary tale about the dangers of allowing negative emotions to drive our actions and the importance of staying true to our faith and values.

On the other hand, we have the example of King David, who also faced moments of self-sabotage. Despite being a man after God's own heart, David succumbed to temptation and committed adultery with Bathsheba, leading to a series of tragic events, including the death of Bathsheba's husband. However, unlike Saul, David showed remorse for his actions and sought forgiveness from God. Through repentance and humility, David overcame his self-sabotaging behavior and rebuilt his relationship with God.

The story of Jonah is another powerful example of self-sabotage in the Bible. When God called Jonah to preach to the people of Nineveh, Jonah initially refused and tried to flee from God's presence. His disobedience led to misfortunes, including being swallowed by a great fish. Eventually, Jonah repented and followed God's command, leading to the salvation of the people of Nineveh. Jonah's story teaches us that running away from our responsibilities and ignoring God's call can only lead to further hardship and suffering.

The Bible is full of examples that illustrate the impact of self-sabotage on our lives. Whether it's through disobedience, insecurity, or fear, self-sabotaging behaviors can have serious consequences that hinder our spiritual and personal growth. By learning from the mistakes of biblical characters and striving to overcome our self-destructive tendencies, we can lead more fulfilling and purposeful lives in alignment with God's will.

Self-sabotage behaviors are frequently embedded, associated with low self-esteem, or functioning as a protection mechanism. We'll discuss the causes of self-sabotage below in more detail.

Typical cases of self-sabotage actions

Fundamentally, self-sabotage harms the people who engage in it. Typical instances of self-sabotage include:

- Procrastination, which is the act of delaying success or preparation.
- Defensiveness (shooing people away or refusing to accept helpful criticism)
- Perfectionism (holding oneself to impossible standards)
- Self-medicating (becoming dependent on drugs or alcohol rather than changing their behavior)

Avoiding people or isolating oneself; asking for aid when needed; picking conflicts or causing trouble in relationships; talking negatively about oneself; ignoring your needs; and overspending.

CHAPTER THREE

IDENTIFYING YOUR SELF-SABOTAGING BEHAVIORS AND PATTERNS

Do you ever feel like something is holding you back from reaching your full potential? Do you find yourself procrastinating on essential responsibilities, doubting your abilities, or avoiding opportunities for growth and success? In this book, these behaviors may be signs of self-sabotage, a common phenomenon that can prevent us from being BOLD, achieving our goals and living our best lives. Self-sabotage occurs when we engage in behaviors that undermine our success or well-being. These behaviors often stem from deep-seated beliefs, fears, or insecurities we may not know. For example, if we believe we are not worthy of success or happiness, we may unconsciously sabotage our efforts to achieve these goals.

Common self-sabotaging behaviors include procrastination, perfectionism, self-doubt, and fear of failure. Procrastination involves putting off important tasks or goals even though we know they are essential for long-term success. Perfectionism involves setting impossibly high standards for ourselves and becoming paralyzed by the fear of not measuring up. Self-doubt and fear of failure can lead us to second-guess ourselves, hesitate to take risks or avoid new opportunities altogether.

Identifying Your Self-Sabotaging Behaviors:

My therapist made this suggestion and I want to share it with you. She told me to start paying attention to my thoughts, feelings, and actions in different situations. Next, notice if I procrastinate when faced with a challenging task or constantly doubt my capabilities. Lastly, reflect on whether I avoid situations that make me uncomfortable or anxious, such as public speaking or networking events. Another way to identify self-sabotaging behaviors is to examine your conversations and the outcome from what you have been allowing out of your mouth.

Everyone occasionally gets in their way. However, those who self-sabotage exhibits a way of thinking and acting inconsistent with what they claim to or want. Studies reveal that those who engage in self-sabotage create problems even when none exist. Although these actions may appear deliberate to others, the self-sabotaging individual may not even know they are engaging in them.

Individuals self-sabotage for various reasons. They can feel unworthy of happiness or achievement and have low self-esteem. It's possible that they picked up unhealthy self-destructive habits as children or from previous relationships. Instead of putting in a lot of effort and seeing if they can achieve their goals, they could undermine their chances out of fear of failure (or success).

According to psychologists, self-sabotage is a way for people to shift the blame for their mistakes. As stated differently, if you undermine your prospects of success, it doesn't count as a failure, and it doesn't have the same negative impact on your self-worth. The specific behaviors of self-sabotage vary widely depending on the individual and the environment. However, those who self-sabotage typically destroys the good things in their lives. They might intentionally harm the good things in their lives or choose not to take the necessary steps. I like to call it "peeing on your lawn." They act in ways that keep them from achieving the goals they claim to have for their lives. Go through them and see if you can identify any of the following frequent indicators of self-defeating behavior.

1. Picking conflict.

Picking conflicts is a typical indicator of relationship self-sabotage. Both friendships and romantic relationships are susceptible to this. Relationship fights and conflicts between people are familiar. Therefore, it's important to remember that having conflict doesn't always indicate self-destructive behavior. However, try to be aware of whether you're the one who starts arguments and whether you do so for reasons that seem insignificant at the time. Picking disputes in this manner may indicate that you are destroying a positive relationship for self-sabotage.

2. Chronic procrastination

There are several possible causes of procrastination, including mental health issues like attention-deficit hyperactivity disorder (ADHD) or obsessive-compulsive disorder (OCD). However, persistently putting off tasks in other situations could indicate self-defeating behavior. One way to lose out on the chance to succeed in a professional endeavor is to put off starting it. If you know that putting off crucial duties will make your life harder down the road, you might do so. You might also put things off because you fear failing or don't think you can achieve.

Finding the cause of your procrastination is crucial since, if you have an underlying mental health issue, you probably require treatment. However, procrastination can occasionally indicate self-sabotage.

3. Giving up before trying

A lot of people self-sabotage just by giving up. They set goals, but instead of working toward them consistently, they constantly alter or give up on them. You can be self-sabotaging if you would sooner give up than continue working toward a goal, particularly after a setback.

Achieving your objectives demands perseverance and dedication. Adjusting your goals as your values evolve is acceptable, but if you give up too soon, you can jeopardize your chances of success.

4. Abusing drugs and alcohol

While not always, drug and alcohol abuse are instances of self-sabotage. Substance abuse is a standard method of self-medication. For instance, individuals may suffer from depression or post-traumatic stress disorder (PTSD), but instead of receiving the necessary treatment, they choose to self-medicate with drugs and alcohol. In these situations, it might be a method of self-defeating. Due to low self-worth or self-esteem, many people with substance use disorders may also self-sabotage. They can be unable to imagine a life free from addiction, which keeps them trapped in the cycle of use.

5. Being overly critical of yourself

Certain forms of self-sabotage involve thought patterns rather than actions. One common technique is being strict with oneself. If you are judgmental and demeaning to yourself, you might be discouraged from pursuing your aspirations. Self-criticism may also keep you from moving forward with your objectives. If you have poor self-esteem, you might convince yourself that you're undeserving of the nice things in your life. This could prompt you to start talking badly to yourself, which is a form of self-sabotage since it undermines your confidence even more.

6. Running from commitments

You may decline to take on significant life responsibilities as a self-sabotage behavior. The age-old example is not wanting to commit to a romantic partner. They might be the ideal match for you, yet your reluctance to commit could cause you to ruin the relationship. Or perhaps you're hesitant to dedicate yourself to a career, which leads you to quit a wonderful job. People are hesitant to commit for various reasons, but if you consistently act this way, it may be an indication of self-sabotage.

7. Being a perfectionist

Perfectionist tendencies are another type of conduct that, while not always indicative of self-sabotage, frequently contribute to it. People with perfectionism tend to set extremely high (and sometimes unachievable) standards for themselves and always strive for perfection. Perfectionism can indicate self-sabotage even though it may seem like a quality that will help you succeed. If you hold yourself to a high standard of perfection, for instance, you could give up on your goals when you fall short of them.

8. Not taking breaks

Similarly, overworking oneself and neglecting to take breaks can be accidental self-sabotage. You may consciously believe that you are exerting yourself to reach your goals. However, in practice, working too much without taking breaks would inevitably result in stress and burnout. Overworking yourself may not seem self-sabotage, but it can harm a bright future.

9. Refusing to seek support

Finally, some individuals self-destruct by refusing to ask for help. Asking for help is always acceptable, regardless of whether you are experiencing a challenging period in your life or have a mental health illness. You risk negatively affecting your relationships, future, and health if you don't ask for or accept help when needed.

Engage in conversation with those around you. Be forceful in communicating to them what you require from them. When you find yourself inclined to speak in a passive-aggressive manner, try to resist the urge—this is also frequently an indication of self-sabotage. Individuals cannot help you unless you express your need for their assistance. These behaviors often stem from internal conflicts, such as fear of failure, low self-esteem, or past traumas. In Christian life, self-sabotage may manifest as doubt, disobedience to God's will, or neglect of spiritual growth. Identifying self-sabotaging behaviors is crucial for personal development and spiritual maturity.

In Proverbs 4:23 (NIV), believers are urged to guard their hearts, recognizing the influence of thoughts and emotions on actions. Similarly, Romans 12:2 (NIV) encourages believers to renew their minds, transforming negative thought patterns and behaviors.

Joseph: Overcoming Self-Doubt and Betrayal

Joseph's story, as recounted in the book of Genesis, provides a powerful example of resilience and

perseverance in the face of self-sabotage. Despite being favored by his father, Jacob, and blessed with prophetic dreams of greatness, Joseph's journey is fraught with challenges and setbacks. His brothers' jealousy and betrayal lead to his enslavement in Egypt, where he faces further trials and temptations. Joseph demonstrates
unwavering faith and resilience throughout his trials, refusing to succumb to self-doubt or bitterness. Despite being unjustly accused and imprisoned, Joseph remains steadfast in his belief in God's plan for his life. His ability to forgive his brothers and rise to power in Egypt showcases his triumph over self-sabotage.

Joseph's story teaches us valuable lessons about resilience, forgiveness, and trust in God's providence. Despite facing numerous setbacks and betrayals, Joseph refuses to allow self-doubt or bitterness to dictate his actions. Instead, he remains faithful to God's plan and ultimately achieves success and redemption.

Moses: Overcoming Self-Doubt and Reluctance

Moses' journey from a reluctant leader to a mighty prophet offers insights into overcoming self-sabotage. When called by God to lead the Israelites out of bondage in Egypt, Moses initially expressed doubt and reluctance. Despite witnessing God's power through miracles and signs, Moses questions his abilities and fears rejection or failure. However, God reassured Moses of His presence and promised to equip him for the task ahead. Through God's guidance and empowerment, Moses overcomes his self-doubt and fulfills his divine calling. Despite facing numerous challenges and obstacles, including resistance from Pharaoh and the Israelites, Moses remains steadfast in his commitment to God's will. Moses' journey reminds us that self-doubt and reluctance are everyday struggles faced by many believers. However, like Moses, we can overcome these obstacles by trusting God's strength and guidance. By relying on God's promises and stepping out in faith, we can conquer self-sabotaging thoughts and achieve our God-given potential.

Jonah: Confronting Fear and Disobedience

Jonah's story highlights the consequences of fear and disobedience in the face of God's calling. When God commands Jonah to preach repentance to the people of Nineveh, Jonah flees in the opposite direction, seeking to escape God's presence and avoid the difficult task ahead. However, Jonah's disobedience leads to trials and tribulations, including being swallowed by a great fish and spending three days in its belly. Through this ordeal, Jonah learns the futility of resisting God's will and the importance of obedience. Eventually, Jonah repents of his disobedience and fulfills his mission to preach repentance to the people of Nineveh.

Jonah's story is a cautionary tale against succumbing to fear and disobedience. By obeying God's commands and trusting in His plan, we can avoid the pitfalls of self-sabotage and experience His blessings and provision.

Identifying Self-Sabotaging Behaviors:

Drawing from the lives of Joseph, Moses, and Jonah, we can identify common self-sabotaging behaviors and patterns:

1. ***Self-Doubt and Fear***: Like Joseph and Moses, individuals may doubt their abilities or fear failure, leading to hesitancy and reluctance to pursue God's calling or goals.

2. ***Disobedience***: Jonah's story illustrates the consequences of disobeying God's commands and seeking to evade His will. Disobedience can lead to trials and setbacks, hindering personal growth and spiritual fulfillment.

3. ***Negative Thought Patterns:*** Self-sabotaging behaviors often stem from negative thoughts, such as self-doubt, criticism, or pessimism. These thoughts can undermine confidence and hinder progress.

4. ***Avoidance and Procrastination:*** Individuals may engage in avoidance behaviors or

procrastination to cope with fear or uncertainty. However, these behaviors can hinder achievement and delay personal growth.

CHAPTER FOUR

YOU'RE THE CASTING DIRECTOR

In the grand theater of life, each individual plays a unique role as the casting director, responsible for shaping their narrative. However, amidst the audition of choices and opportunities, fear often emerges as a formidable actor, ready to take center stage and influence our decisions. Fear, a primal emotion rooted in uncertainty and anticipation of danger, can influence our thoughts, feelings, and actions. When left unchecked, anxiety can manifest as self-sabotage, sabotaging our dreams, relationships, and potential for growth. Self-sabotage, often fueled by fear of failure, rejection, or inadequacy, leads individuals to undermine their success and well-being. As the casting director of your life, you can choose the roles that fear plays in your story. Fear can often lead to self-sabotage, holding us back from reaching our full potential and achieving our goals. This chapter will explore how fear can influence our actions and decisions, leading to self-sabotaging behaviors. We will also examine relevant Bible passages that offer guidance and encouragement to overcome fear and break free from the cycle of self-sabotage.

Fear is a common emotion that can manifest in various forms, such as fear of failure, rejection, or the unknown. When we allow fear to take center stage in our lives, it can paralyze us and prevent us from taking risks or pursuing our dreams. This fear-based mindset can lead us to engage in self-sabotaging behaviors, such as procrastination, negative self-talk, or avoidance of challenges.

Fear influences self-sabotage by creating a sense of doubt and insecurity in our abilities. We may question our worthiness, skills, or capabilities, leading us to undermine ourselves and sabotage our success. This self-doubt can stem from past experiences, negative beliefs about ourselves, or external pressures and expectations. in Isaiah 41:10, the Bible says, "Fear not, for I am with you; be not dismayed, for I am your God; I will strengthen you, I will help you, I will uphold you with my righteous right hand." This verse reminds us that God is always by our side, offering strength, support, and guidance in times of fear and uncertainty. By trusting God's promises, we can overcome fear and resist the urge to sabotage ourselves. and 2 Timothy 1:7 confirms this to us, which states, ***"For God gave us a spirit not of fear but of power and love and self-control."*** This passage emphasizes that fear is not from God and does not align with His plan for us. Instead, God has equipped us with power, love, and self-control, enabling us to conquer fear and break free from self-sabotaging patterns.

When fear threatens to derail our progress and sabotage our efforts, we can turn to God for strength and courage. By seeking His guidance through prayer, meditation, and reflection on His word, we can combat fear and replace self-sabotaging thoughts with faith, hope, and perseverance. With God's support and presence in our lives, we can rewrite our story, casting out fear and embracing a role filled with confidence, resilience, and purpose.

Joseph: Confronting Fear of Rejection and Betrayal

The story of Joseph, found in the Book of Genesis, offers profound insights into overcoming fear and resisting self-sabotage. Despite being favored by his father, Jacob, Joseph's brothers' jealousy, and betrayal led to his enslavement in Egypt. Throughout his journey, Joseph confronts his fear of rejection, abandonment, and injustice. Despite facing numerous trials and setbacks, Joseph remains steadfast in his faith and refuses to succumb to fear's grip. His unwavering trust in God's plan enables him to overcome adversity and fulfill his divine purpose. Genesis 50:20 (NIV) encapsulates Joseph's resilience, as he declares, "You intended to harm me, but God intended it for good to accomplish what is now being done, the saving of many lives."

Moses: Overcoming Fear of Inadequacy and Rejection

Moses' reluctance to heed God's call to lead the Israelites out of Egypt reflects the influence of fear on self-sabotage. Despite witnessing God's miraculous signs and assurances of His presence, Moses doubts his ability to fulfill the task. In Exodus 4:10 (NIV), Moses expresses his fear of inadequacy, stating, "Pardon your servant, Lord. I have never been eloquent, neither in the past nor since you have spoken to your servant. I am slow of speech and tongue."

However, God reassures Moses of His presence and promises to equip him for the journey ahead. Exodus 4:12 (NIV) affirms God's provision, as He declares, "Now go; I will help you speak and will teach you what to say." Despite his initial fears, Moses eventually embraces his role as a leader and delivers the Israelites from bondage, demonstrating the power of faith over fear.

Jonah: Confronting Fear of Failure and Disobedience

Jonah's reluctance to obey God's command to preach repentance to the people of Nineveh illustrates the destructive influence of fear on self-sabotage. Fearing failure and rejection, Jonah attempts to flee from God's presence, boarding a ship bound for Tarshish. However, God intervenes, sending a great storm redirecting Jonah's path.

Despite his attempts to evade God's will, Jonah ultimately confronts his fear and obeys God's command to preach to the people of Nineveh. His message of repentance leads to widespread revival, highlighting the transformative power of overcoming fear and embracing obedience.

Identifying Fear-Based Self-Sabotage:

Fear-based self-sabotage can manifest in various ways, hindering personal growth and fulfillment. Common signs include:

1. ***Avoidance of Opportunities:*** Fear of failure or rejection may lead individuals to avoid pursuing opportunities for growth or advancement.

2. ***Procrastination:*** Fear of inadequacy or perfectionism may result in procrastination, delaying progress and undermining success.

3. ***Negative Self-Talk:*** Fear-based self-sabotage often manifests as negative self-talk, undermining confidence and reinforcing feelings of unworthiness.

4. ***Resistance to Change***: Fear of the unknown or discomfort may lead individuals to resist change, perpetuating stagnation and hindering personal development.

The story of Naomi from the Bible provides a powerful illustration of how fear can lead to self-sabotage and how faith and trust in God can bring redemption and restoration. Naomi's journey is a testament to the transformative power of overcoming fear with faith and resilience. Through her experiences, we can glean valuable lessons on navigating the challenges of anxiety and self-sabotage in our lives. Naomi faced numerous trials and hardships in her life. In the book of Ruth, we learn that Naomi and her family left their homeland of Bethlehem during famine and settled in Moab. Tragically, Naomi's husband passed away, leaving her a widow with her two sons, Mahlon and Chilion. Eventually, her sons also died, leaving Naomi devastated and alone with her daughters-in-law, Orpah and Ruth.

Naomi's grief and loss led her to a place of deep despair and hopelessness. In her sorrow, she felt abandoned by God and questioned the purpose of her suffering. This fear and hopelessness caused Naomi to see herself as cursed and unworthy of God's favor. In her anguish, Naomi believed that her life was marked by tragedy and that there was no hope for a better future.

Naomi's self-sabotaging thoughts and beliefs clouded her vision and prevented her from seeing the possibilities for redemption and restoration. Fueled by fear and despair, Naomi returned to Bethlehem, urging her daughters-in-law to stay in Moab and seek new husbands. Orpah chose to remain in Moab, but Ruth clung to Naomi, declaring her loyalty and commitment to accompany her back to Bethlehem. Despite Naomi's initial reluctance and despair, Ruth's unwavering devotion and faithfulness became a beacon of hope and light in Naomi's darkness. Through Ruth's steadfast love and loyalty, Naomi began to see glimpses of God's grace and provision in her life. As they journeyed back to Bethlehem, Naomi's heart slowly started to soften, and she began to recognize how God was at work in her midst. Upon returning to Bethlehem, Naomi's perspective began to shift as she witnessed the unfolding of God's plan through Ruth. Through a series of remarkable events, Ruth found favor in the eyes of Boaz, a wealthy landowner who showed kindness and generosity to Ruth and Naomi. Boaz ultimately redeemed Ruth and Naomi, restoring their dignity and providing for their needs.

Through Ruth's faithfulness, God transformed Naomi's fear and despair into hope and joy. Naomi's story is a powerful reminder that even in our darkest moments, God is present and working behind the scenes to bring healing and restoration. By trusting in God's faithfulness and leaning on the support of others, we can overcome the grip of fear and self-sabotage in our lives.

Just as Naomi experienced redemption and restoration through Ruth's faithfulness and God's providence, we, too, can find strength and courage to confront our fears and break free from self-sabotaging patterns. By nurturing a deep faith in God's promises and surrounding ourselves with supportive companions on our journey, we can rewrite our stories and embrace a narrative filled with hope, resilience, and victory. Naomi's story illuminates the profound impact of fear and self-sabotage on our lives and the transformative power of faith and trust in God. Through Naomi's journey, we learn that God's light shines through even in our darkest moments, offering us hope and redemption.

What of a Job? He said, What I feared has come upon me; what I dreaded has happened to me. Job 3:25. The story of Job is a profound tale of suffering, faith, and resilience that offers valuable insights into how we can navigate fear and self-sabotage in our lives. Job's experiences are a powerful example of how unwavering trust in God's goodness and sovereignty can help us overcome adversity and emerge stronger on the other side. Through Job's story, we can glean important lessons on confronting fear, overcoming self-sabotage, and finding hope amid trials.

Job was a man of great wealth and moral integrity who lived in the land of Uz. He enjoyed a prosperous life with a loving family and abundant blessings from God. However, Job's faith and character were tested when he faced a series of devastating trials that shook the very foundation of his existence. In a short period, Job lost everything he held dear – wealth, children, and health. Afflicted by painful sores and enduring the scorn of his friends and loved ones, Job plunged into a bottomless pit of despair and anguish. The weight of his suffering became unbearable, and he was consumed by questions of why God would allow such calamity to befall him. In the depths of his despair, Job grappled with fear and self-doubt. He questioned his worthiness and righteousness, wondering if his suffering was a punishment for past sins or a sign of God's abandonment. Job's inner turmoil and struggle with self-sabotaging thoughts threatened to overwhelm him, leading him to cry out in despair and agony.

Despite his anguish, Job clung to his faith in God's goodness and justice. He refused to turn away from believing in God's sovereignty and steadfast love, even in the face of seemingly insurmountable adversity. Job's unwavering trust in God's character and promises became a lifeline in his darkest hour, sustaining him through the storm of suffering and doubt. As Job wrestled with his fears and self-sabotaging thoughts, he found solace in his friends' companionship, who offered comfort and counsel. Though their words sometimes missed the mark and added to his distress, Job's interactions with his friends reminded him of the importance of community and support in times of trial.

Through his conversations with his friends and introspection, Job began to find peace and clarity amidst the chaos of his circumstances. He gained newfound insights into the mystery of suffering and the complexities of human existence, leading him to a deeper understanding of God's ways and purposes.

Amid his suffering, Job's faith was tested like never before. He faced the temptation to curse God and give in to despair, but instead, he chose to cling to his belief in God's goodness and faithfulness. Job's resilience in the face of trials is an inspiring example of how we can confront our fears and overcome self-sabotaging tendencies through unwavering faith and trust in God.

God's grace and mercy shone brightly in his life as Job persevered through his ordeal with patience and perseverance. In a remarkable display of divine restoration, God healed Job's physical afflictions and blessed him with even greater abundance and prosperity than before. Job's story is a testament to the redemptive power of faith and the triumph of hope over despair. Through Job's journey of suffering and restoration, we learn that even in our darkest moments, God is present and at work in our lives. By following Job's example of unwavering faith and trust in God's goodness, we can confront our fears, overcome self-sabotage, and emerge robust and resilient on the other side.

What, then, can be done to prevent self-sabotage? Here are twelve strategies to overcome your fear and move forward:

1. ***Being conscious***. Acknowledge that fear, in whatever form it may appear, is the cause of the self-sabotage. Gaining insight into the circumstances enables you to comprehend yourself more fully.

2. **Name it.** Do you fear failing, succeeding, or both? Is it a fear of what people will say? Are you terrified because you are vulnerable? Fearful of emotion? Fearful of suffering harm? Naming helps deflect some of the power away from the source of your dread.

3. ***Clearly define your "why."*** Do you want your mother to be proud of you finally, or are you writing a book because you love words? Do you want to reduce weight to feel better about yourself or so that other people will find you attractive? Be very explicit about the reasons behind any aspiration or objective. Furthermore, if your dream or objective doesn't come from

within you but is someone else's, it truly doesn't belong to you.

4. ***Take a single, tiny step***. To overcome your fear, take the next step toward your objective rather than leaping off a cliff into the water.

5. **Build up your bravery muscles**. By taking on your worries, you can develop confidence in yourself.

6. ***Include action in everyday activities.*** Although routines may seem monotonous, you will feel less afraid to incorporate your goals into your daily activities intentionally. The added benefit is less distance when you behave according to your desires.

7. ***Understand what is not negotiable.*** Put your daily non-negotiables on paper to position yourself for success.

8. ***Recognize the causes.*** What has historically caused self-sabotage? Is it a specific Facebook "friend"? Does talking about your sister's ideal

life make sense? Does it mean it's hungry or getting too little sleep?

9. ***Be aware of your tricks.*** When we sabotage ourselves, we can halt ourselves in our tracks. Get enough sleep, eat healthful foods, and drink lots of water to give your life more energy.

10. ***Turn off the guilt.*** Talk about your anxieties with someone you can trust. Our shame is silenced when we face it head-on.

11. ***Take responsibility.*** Employ a mentor. Exercise with a companion. Engage in a sincere dialogue with your significant other.

CHAPTER FIVE

WATCH YOUR MOUTH" OVERCOMING NEGATIVE SELF-TALK AND LIMITING BELIEFS

Death and life are in the power of the tongue,
And those who love it will eat its fruit.
Proverbs 18:21.

Sometime back, I was reading the prophet Jeremiah's book, and I was impressed by the opening conversation between God and the young prophet: Now the word of the Lord came to me, saying, "Before I formed you in the womb, I knew you, and before you were born, I consecrated you; I appointed you a prophet to the nations." Then I said, "Ah, Lord God! Behold, I do not know how to speak, for I am only a youth." But the Lord told me, "Do not say, I am only a youth; for to all I send you, you shall go, and whatever

I command you, you shall speak. Do not be afraid of them, for I am with you to deliver you, declares the Lord." - Jeremiah 1:4-8 ESV

How often does God speak to us about the good works He's prepared for us to do before the foundation of the world (Eph 2:10), and we have the same response as Jeremiah?

"Ah, Lord. Have you noticed my weaknesses? I need to be stronger. I'm too old. I need to be younger. I need more experience. I also am. We fill in the gap by using whatever self-limiting factors we have been letting keep us back for a while. In return, God says, "Stop talking in self-limiting words!" Then, He addresses the actual problem by saying, "Do not be afraid of them; I am here to deliver you."

The boundaries that we place on ourselves stem from fear. Dread of failing to succeed. Fear of being exposed as forgers. Fear of our shortcomings. Fear of the words or actions of others. We talk to ourselves more than anybody else does. We are in charge of our dialogue with ourselves. How's that talk going?

Limiting language can keep you from the life you were meant to live. Let's explore how our use of language can inadvertently limit our thinking and hold us back from reaching our full potential.

The story of Elisha and the Shunammite woman, found in 2 Kings 4:8-37, is a powerful example of how our words and beliefs can impact our lives. This story teaches valuable lessons on overcoming negative self-talk and limiting beliefs to achieve growth and blessings in our journey. In the biblical narrative, Elisha is a prophet known for performing miracles and acts of God's power. The Shunammite woman, on the other hand, was a generous and kind-hearted woman who shows hospitality to Elisha by providing him with food and shelter whenever he passes through her town. Impressed by her generosity, Elisha wants to show his Gratitude and bless her in return. One day, Elisha asked the Shunammite woman what he could do for her as a token of appreciation for her generosity. She replied that she was content with her life and had no special requests. However, Elisha's servant Gehazi noticed that the woman had no children and suggested that Elisha bless her with a child. At first, the Shunammite woman was hesitant and expressed doubts about possibly having a child at her age. She had likely internalized the belief that she was too old to conceive and bear a child. Despite her initial skepticism, Elisha assured her she would have a son within a year. True to Elisha's word, the Shunammite woman miraculously conceived and gave birth to a son. However, tragedy struck when her son suddenly fell ill and died. In her grief and despair, the Shunammite woman turned to Elisha for help. With unwavering faith, she approached the prophet and expressed her anguish, clinging to the Hope that Elisha could intercede on her behalf. Elisha, moved by the woman's distress, revived her son. Through God's power working through him, Elisha brought the boy back to life, restoring joy and hope to the Shunammite woman's heart. The miraculous restoration of her son served as a testament to the power of Faith and the importance of believing in the possibility of miracles, even in the face of overwhelming odds.

From the story of Elisha and the Shunammite woman, God shows us critical insights on the theme of overcoming negative self-talk and limiting beliefs:

1. ***Mind Your Words:*** The Shunammite woman initially doubted the possibility of having a child due to her advanced age. Her negative self-talk and limiting beliefs hindered her from believing in the extraordinary blessings within her reach. Being mindful of our words to ourselves and others is essential, as our speech can empower or limit us.

2. ***Challenge Your Beliefs:*** When confronted with limiting beliefs, it is crucial to challenge and question them. The Shunammite woman's doubt about bearing a child was based on societal norms and her perceptions of what was possible. By daring to challenge her beliefs and opening herself up to the possibility of a miracle, she experienced a profound transformation in her life.

3. ***Cultivate Your Faith:*** Despite facing adversity and loss, the Shunammite woman's unwavering Faith in Elisha and God's power sustained her through the darkest moments. By nurturing a steadfast belief in the goodness and provision of

a higher power, we can strengthen our Resilience and courage to overcome obstacles and achieve breakthroughs in our lives.

4. ***Seek Support and Guidance:*** Just as the Shunammite woman turned to Elisha for help in her time of need, it is essential that we don't become prideful. It's so important to seek support and guidance from trusted mentors, friends, or spiritual advisors when we are faced with challenges. Surrounding ourselves with positive influences and seeking wise counsel can give us the encouragement and assistance needed to navigate difficult circumstances.

5. ***Embrace Hope:*** The miraculous restoration of the Shunammite woman's son is a beacon of Hope and inspiration. No matter how dire or hopeless a situation may seem, there is always room for miracles and divine intervention. By holding onto Hope and believing in the possibility of transformation, we can overcome despair and find renewed purpose and joy in our lives.

6. ***Practice Gratitude***: The Shunammite woman's generosity towards Elisha and her willingness to extend hospitality without expecting anything in return exemplify the importance of cultivating a spirit of Gratitude. By appreciating the blessings, we have and expressing thankfulness for the goodness in our lives, we shift our focus from lack to abundance, fostering a mindset of positivity and enrichment.

7. ***Be Resilient:*** Despite facing setbacks and challenges, the Shunammite woman demonstrated resilience and perseverance in her journey. Her ability to overcome adversity with grace and Faith serves as a reminder that Resilience is key to navigating life's ups and downs. By embracing resilience and bouncing back from setbacks, we strengthen our character and resolve to face future obstacles with courage and determination. You are stronger than you think!

8. ***Learn from Setbacks:*** The loss of the Shunammite woman's son was a heartbreaking

event that tested her Faith and resolve. However, through this trial, she learned valuable lessons about trust, surrender, and the Resilience of the human spirit. Setbacks and failures can serve as opportunities for growth and self-discovery, shaping us into stronger, more compassionate individuals capable of overcoming even the most difficult circumstances.

9. ***Celebrate Victories***: The miraculous restoration of the Shunammite woman's son was a cause for celebration and rejoicing. It reminded her that no situation is beyond redemption and that victory can emerge from despair. Celebrating our successes, no matter how small reinforces our belief in our capabilities and fuels our motivation to continue striving toward our goals with unwavering determination.

10. ***Share Your Story***: Just as the story of Elisha and the Shunammite woman has inspired countless individuals throughout history, sharing our stories of triumph over adversity can inspire and uplift others facing similar challenges. By

sharing our experiences with vulnerability and authenticity, we create connections, foster empathy, and offer Hope to those who need encouragement and support.

Are you aware that God has exalted YOU with honor and glory? Do you accept this as fact, or do you let your previous failures and present difficulties shape how you see yourself? Are you undervaluing the honor and glory that God Himself intended for YOU to bear in your life as a bearer of HIS image?

The Bible says a lot about what comes out of our mouths. The power of the tongue determines one's life or death. We honor our Lord and Father with our tongues and words, and we curse those who are fashioned in God's image—possibly more than anyone—with them. Blessings and curses issue from the same mouth. My brothers, this shouldn't be the case.

Death and life are in the power of the tongue, and those who love it will eat its fruit. Proverbs 18:21

CHAPTER SIX

BUILDING SELF-AWARENESS AND MINDFULNESS TO COMBAT SELF-SABOTAGE

Developing self-awareness is one of the most important first stages in recognizing self-sabotaging behavior. Introspection, or self-awareness, is essential for identifying harmful behavioral patterns and fortifying one's capacity to interrupt them. "I keep doing (behavior), but I want to achieve (goal)." I might remark, "I want to get a passport, but I keep missing the appointment," as an example. Now that I know what the behavior is and how I continue to stop it, I can search for new contexts in which it might occur. For instance, I might discover that I never schedule appointments for my passport or frequently miss doctor's appointments. You'll become aware of your habits once you begin asking yourself these questions—and they may appear in more than one aspect of your life. The following are a few common examples of self-defeating behavior patterns:

1. Perfectionism

Although aiming for perfection may seem admirable, it frequently prevents one from being functional. Perfectionists often find it challenging to begin projects, and even when they do, their fixation with the specifics prevents them from completing them. Also, those prone to all-or-nothing thinking are perfectionists. Before they even begin, they talk themselves out of possible chances and tend to be very hard on themselves.

2. Moderation

Those who have trouble with moderation frequently have trouble establishing limits. They may appear to be people-pleasing in this behavior, which leads them to say "yes" to too many requests. Alternatively, it could be an excess of alcohol consumed on a night out or a lack of moderation in other parts of their lives. Other, more subdued methods of "overdoing it" include working out at the gym until you are exhausted or staying up late watching TV. Overcommitting frequently hides an underlying fear of failure, even if it may appear to be a strong will to succeed.

3. Running on empty

The story of the goose that laid the golden egg may be familiar. The owner cut open the goose to obtain all the eggs since they were sick of only receiving one a day, but things didn't turn out well. It's not only naive to disregard your personal needs in an attempt to accomplish more; it's a subtle form of self-sabotage.

4. Procrastination

Everyone has occasionally put off doing something, especially if it's a task they could be more excited about. However, delaying your obligations may indeed be a sign of low confidence. When you put off doing it, you deprive yourself of the time and resources necessary to complete your finest work. Perfectionism and procrastination frequently coexist. When perfectionists believe they can't complete a task flawlessly, they often put it off.

5. Lack of communication

You know you need help with a project but choose not to ask for it. Even though you're running late, you decide not to text. Our lives involve constant communication, both at work and outside of it. Our inability to communicate is frequently the result of self-criticism. We fear that we are drawing attention to our shortcomings by seeking assistance. Unfortunately, poor communication can be damaging to our interpersonal bonds. Even worse, it might foster an environment where impostor syndrome thrives. You live in constant terror of being "found out" because nobody knows what you're going through.

Understanding oneself is akin to navigating through uncharted waters in personal growth and development. It requires a compass, a guiding light that illuminates the depths of our thoughts, emotions, and actions. Self-awareness and mindfulness serve as this guiding light, helping individuals navigate the turbulent seas of self-sabotage towards calmer shores of self-realization and success.

6. The Power of Self-Awareness

Self-awareness is the cornerstone of personal growth. It involves recognizing and understanding one's thoughts, emotions, behaviors, strengths, and weaknesses without judgment. By cultivating self-awareness, individuals gain insight into their patterns of self-sabotage and the underlying reasons driving these behaviors.

7. Practicing Self-Reflection

Self-reflection is a powerful tool for building self-awareness. It involves setting aside time to examine one's thoughts, feelings, and actions introspectively. Through journaling, meditation, or quiet contemplation, individuals can gain clarity about their motivations, fears, and limiting beliefs contributing to self-sabotage.

8. Seeking Feedback

Feedback from others can provide valuable insights into blind spots and areas for growth. By soliciting honest feedback from trusted friends, mentors, or coaches, individuals can gain a different perspective on their behavior and its impact on their goals. This external perspective can help uncover patterns of self-sabotage that may have gone unnoticed.

9. Embracing Vulnerability

Vulnerability is often seen as a weakness but is a cornerstone of authentic self-awareness. Individuals create space for self-discovery and growth by embracing vulnerability and acknowledging imperfections. It requires courage to confront the parts of ourselves that we may not be proud of, but it is essential for overcoming self-sabotage and fostering genuine personal development.

10. Cultivating Mindfulness

Mindfulness is the practice of being present in the moment with full awareness and acceptance of one's thoughts, feelings, and sensations. It is a powerful antidote to the autopilot mode that often fuels self-sabotage. By cultivating mindfulness, individuals can develop greater clarity, emotional resilience, and self-regulation, essential for overcoming self-sabotaging behaviors.

11. Practicing Mindful Awareness

Mindful awareness involves paying attention to the present moment with openness and curiosity, without judgment. By observing thoughts and emotions as they arise, individuals can cultivate a greater sense of control over their reactions and behaviors. Mindfulness techniques such as mindful breathing, body scans, and sensory awareness can help anchor individuals in the present moment and reduce the impulse to engage in self-sabotage.

12. Developing Emotional Regulation

Emotional regulation is managing and responding to emotions healthily and constructively. Mindfulness practices such as meditation and deep breathing can help individuals develop greater emotional resilience and self-control. By observing emotions without becoming overwhelmed, individuals can avoid reactive behaviors that often lead to self-sabotage.

13. Cultivating Compassion

Self-compassion is an essential component of mindfulness that involves treating oneself with kindness, understanding, and acceptance, especially in the face of failure or adversity. By cultivating self-compassion, individuals can overcome feelings of inadequacy and self-criticism that contribute to self-sabotage. It involves recognizing that everyone experiences setbacks and mistakes and offering oneself the same kindness and support one would provide a friend.

14. Integrating Self-Awareness and Mindfulness

While self-awareness and mindfulness are potent practices, their true potential is realized when integrated into daily life. By combining self-awareness with mindfulness, individuals can deeply understand their inner landscape and cultivate the resources necessary to overcome self-sabotage.

15. Daily Mindfulness Practices

Incorporating mindfulness practices into daily routines can help reinforce self-awareness and promote emotional well-being. Simple activities such as mindful breathing, mindful eating, or taking mindful walks can help individuals stay grounded in the present moment and cultivate a sense of inner peace and balance.

16. Reflective Journaling

Journaling is a powerful tool for integrating self-awareness into your daily life. By writing down thoughts, emotions, and experiences, individuals can gain clarity about their inner world and identify patterns of self-sabotage. Regular journaling can also serve as a form of self-reflection and self-expression, that helps deepen your understanding of yourself and your triggers for self-sabotage.

17. Mindful Decision-Making

Mindful decision-making involves making conscious choices based on present-moment awareness and self-reflection. By pausing to consider the potential consequences of their actions and aligning them with their values and goals, individuals can avoid impulsive behaviors that lead to self-sabotage. Mindful decision-making also involves being open to feedback and learning from past mistakes, allowing individuals to course-correct and grow from their experiences.

If you want to feel better about yourself, it will be worth your effort to learn to trust yourself again. However, where do you even begin? Maintaining your word is one of the most straightforward strategies. Over time, these minor positive self-interactions can help you feel more capable and in control of your fate, even if you make the most minor promises to yourself. Further, it can help you erase any unfavorable thoughts or sentiments about yourself and provide the clarity you need to realize that you are not your mistakes. Creating a secure environment to support your inner self is the first step towards improving yourself.

CHAPTER SEVEN

STRATEGIES FOR BREAKING THE CYCLE OF SELF-SABOTAGE

Self-sabotage is like stumbling over our own feet while trying to walk forward. It's frustrating and confusing and often leaves us wondering why we keep getting in our way. But breaking free from the cycle of self-sabotage is possible. By understanding the patterns that hold us back and implementing effective strategies, we can reclaim control of our lives and move towards our goals confidently and clearly. In this guide, we'll explore simple yet powerful techniques for breaking the cycle of self-sabotage and cultivating a life filled with success, fulfillment, and self-empowerment.

1. ***Identifying Patterns***: The first step in breaking the cycle of self-sabotage is to identify the patterns that keep us stuck. This may involve

reflecting on past experiences, examining our thought patterns and behaviors, and seeking feedback from others. By recognizing the recurring themes and triggers that lead to self-sabotage, we can begin to interrupt these patterns and create space for new, more empowering behaviors.

2. ***Exploring Underlying Beliefs:*** Self-sabotage often stems from limiting beliefs about ourselves and our abilities. These beliefs may be rooted in past experiences, societal conditioning, or negative self-talk. By exploring and challenging these beliefs, we can start to shift our mindset from one of self-doubt to one of self-empowerment. Affirmations, positive self-talk, and cognitive-behavioral techniques can be helpful tools in this process.

3. ***Strategies for Breaking the Cycle:*** Breaking free from the cycle of self-sabotage requires a combination of self-awareness, self-compassion, and concrete action steps. Here are some simple yet effective strategies for overcoming self-

sabotage and moving toward a life of fulfillment and success:

4. ***Cultivate Self-Awareness:*** Self-awareness is the foundation of personal growth and change. By becoming more aware of our thoughts, emotions, and behaviors, we can understand the underlying drivers of self-sabotage and take proactive steps toward change. Mindfulness practices such as meditation, journaling, and self-reflection can help cultivate self-awareness and create space for greater clarity and insight.

5. ***Practice Self-Compassion:*** Self-sabotage often thrives in an environment of self-criticism and judgment. By practicing self-compassion, we can learn to treat ourselves with kindness and understanding, especially in the face of setbacks and challenges. Self-compassion involves recognizing that we are human and that we all make mistakes. It means offering ourselves the same care and support that we would provide to a friend in need.

6. ***Set Realistic Goals:*** Setting unrealistic or overly ambitious goals can set us up for failure and reinforce feelings of inadequacy and self-doubt. Instead, focus on setting small, achievable goals that align with your values and priorities. Celebrate your progress along the way and be willing to adjust your goals as needed. Setting realistic goals can build momentum and confidence as you work towards your larger aspirations.

7. ***Break Tasks into Manageable Steps:*** Feeling overwhelmed can often lead to procrastination and avoidance, fueling the cycle of self-sabotage. Break larger tasks or projects into smaller, more manageable steps, and focus on tackling one step at a time. This can help make the task more manageable and reduce overwhelm and anxiety. Celebrate each small victory, no matter how small, and use it as motivation to keep moving forward.

8. ***Practice Self-Regulation:*** Self-regulation involves managing impulses, emotions, and

behaviors in line with our goals and values. This means recognizing when we engage in self-sabotaging behaviors and taking proactive steps to course correct. Techniques such as deep breathing, visualization, and positive self-talk can help regulate emotions and promote a sense of calm and clarity in the face of challenges.

Breaking free from the cycle of self-sabotage doesn't have to be a solo journey:

1. **Reach out to trusted friends, family members, mentors, or therapists for support and encouragement.** My personal experience since 2020 has been the not just the most humbling but the most liberating. It wasn't until I started therapy was I able to become aware of my self-sabotaging behaviors. I'm eternally grateful for the support I have from my therapist and my circle. Surround yourself with people who believe in you and your abilities and can provide guidance and perspective when needed. Remember that asking for help is a sign of

strength, not weakness and that we all need support from time to time.

2. **Practice Self-Care**. Self-care is essential for maintaining emotional and mental well-being, especially when breaking free from the cycle of self-sabotage. Make time for activities that nourish your body, mind, and spirit, whether exercising in nature, practicing hobbies, or simply taking a break to rest and recharge. Remember that self-care is not selfish but a necessary investment in your health and happiness.

3. **Set Clear Goals and Action Plans.** Setting clear, achievable goals and creating action plans to achieve them is essential for breaking the cycle of self-sabotage. Individuals can stay focused, motivated, and accountable by defining specific, measurable, realistic, and time-bound objectives. Breaking down larger goals into smaller, manageable tasks makes the process less overwhelming and increases the likelihood of success.

4. **Develop Healthy Habits and Routines.** Healthy habits and routines can help individuals overcome self-sabotage and foster positive change. Regular exercise, proper nutrition, restful sleep, mindfulness practices, and social connections contribute to overall well-being and resilience. Creating a daily routine with self-care activities and meaningful pursuits can enhance motivation, productivity, and self-esteem.

5. **Seek Support and Accountability.** Breaking the cycle of self-sabotage can be challenging, but individuals do not have to navigate this journey alone. Seeking support from friends, family members, mentors, therapists, or support groups can provide encouragement, guidance, and accountability. Sharing struggles and victories with others can help individuals stay motivated, gain new perspectives, and build a strong support network.

6. **Embrace Failure and Learn from Mistakes.** Failure is a natural part of the growth process and should be viewed as an opportunity for

learning and growth rather than a reflection of one's worth or abilities. By embracing failure and reframing mistakes as valuable lessons, individuals can develop resilience, adaptability, and a growth mindset. Reflecting on past failures, identifying lessons learned, and applying insights to future endeavors can help individuals break free from self-sabotaging behaviors.

7. **Practice Self-Compassion and Forgiveness.** Self-compassion involves treating oneself with kindness, understanding, and acceptance, especially in times of difficulty or setback. Individuals can counteract self-criticism, perfectionism, and harsh judgment that fuel self-sabotage by cultivating self-compassion. Forgiving oneself for past mistakes and shortcomings is crucial for letting go of guilt, shame, and self-blame and moving forward with courage and compassion.

8. **Celebrate Successes and Milestones.** Acknowledging and celebrating small victories,

progress, and milestones along the way is essential for breaking the cycle of self-sabotage. By recognizing and rewarding accomplishments, individuals can boost their confidence, motivation, and sense of achievement. Celebrating success—whether big or small—reinforces positive behaviors, builds momentum, and reminds individuals of their strengths and capabilities. Reflecting on achievements and expressing gratitude for progress can inspire continued growth and resilience.

9. **Practice Cultivating a Growth Mindset**. A growth mindset involves believing in one's capacity to learn, grow, and improve rather than seeing abilities as fixed traits. By cultivating a growth mindset, individuals can approach challenges with curiosity, resilience, and a willingness to experiment and adapt. Embracing feedback, seeking growth opportunities, and viewing setbacks as steppingstones toward success can help individuals break free from

self-sabotaging behaviors and unlock their full potential.

Breaking the cycle of self-sabotage will require you having courage, commitment, and a willingness to confront and transform negative patterns. By applying the strategies outlined in this section - cultivating self-awareness, practicing mindfulness, challenging negative beliefs, setting clear goals, developing healthy habits, seeking support, embracing failure, practicing self-compassion, celebrating successes, and cultivating a growth mindset - individuals can overcome self-sabotaging tendencies and create a more fulfilling and purposeful life. Change takes time, effort, and patience, but with dedication and perseverance, breaking free from self-sabotage is possible. Stay focused on your goals, be kind to yourself, and trust in your ability to create positive life changes. You deserve to live a life free from self-imposed limitations and full of growth, joy, and success.

CHAPTER 8

SELF-COMPASSION: GIVE YOURSELF SOME GRACE

Self-care refers to how we intentionally care for ourselves—our physical, mental, and emotional wellbeing. Just like the battery on our phone, we require recharging. You drive your life. It will only serve you well if you don't maintain it and keep the engine fed. Reviving yourself is achieved through self-care. It facilitates rest. It enables you to move on from tense situations. It provides you with the viewpoint you require to manage your days. Above all, it allows you to take care of other people.

Self-compassion is the foundation of self-care. Maintaining self-care habits is easier if you have compassion for yourself. You tend to think intuitively that you don't deserve the attention if you lack self-compassion. Looking at your difficulties with respect and understanding is compassionate. Giving yourself the benefit of the doubt is an act of compassion. Acknowledging that you tried your hardest is an act of compassion. Individually and collectively, self-compassion and self-care must be a significant part of your daily practices if you are to successfully navigate the difficulties of living and working in stressful times. These five practice tips can help you cultivate self-compassion and self-care daily.

1. Be intentional about your self-care

Regular times can quickly push self-care routines aside from our lives. They may become even more marginalized and overpowered during stressful situations. An intentional mentality and action plan allow you to consider self-care a vital aspect of your life. Encourage your intentionality by thinking back to the things that make you happy, relaxed, or refreshed. After that, include those activities in your new routines. Examine your previous beliefs about self-care in your new, more demanding situation. When specific times, places, or activities aren't available, consider alternative and innovative approaches to the "how" and "when" of your self-care. For instance, your new circumstances might force you to run at a time you would have thought to be an option only if you enjoy doing so in the morning.

2. Surface and replace negative thoughts about yourself

Maintaining self-compassion and self-care is challenging if a constant stream of unfavorable ideas about your situation or yourself plagues you. Furthermore, these unfavorable thought patterns can become self-reinforcing in your mind. It is to bring those negative thoughts to the surface and replace them. Some might exist on a conscious, day-to-day basis, and others might be more of your life's unspoken subtext. In any case, you will need to intentionally reflect to bring them to light and create a fresh, more optimistic internal story.

To start, practice mindfulness to identify such negative thoughts. Jot them down without editing, and then give your notes some thought. Next, purposefully swap them out for more sympathetic and kind words. Think of yourself as a buddy who is requesting warmer and gentler perspectives. How would you advise them?

3. Actively reframe your thinking and choices

An excellent illustration of opting for a new perspective is a caregiver's experience at work amid a crisis. From the outside, we might notice the danger and difficulty, but the caregiver might recognize the bravery in the struggle of the people they look after. Instead of seeing hardship, they have chosen to see courage. We may all participate in this kind of change by posing questions like "How can I reframe my thinking?" or "What is another view of the situation?". Another viewpoint is always available. Sometimes, all it takes to find it is humility and thoughtful discipline. "Yes" is one way to reframe the situation. Also, indeed, I fell short of my target today. And I did have a few significant talks." "Yes, I am stressed and tired after having the kids home all day. Likewise, we are interacting and playing more than I ever imagined." "He does interrupt frequently. And he has a strong enthusiasm for the subject."

4. Think of yourself as an explorer in a new situation

This is a particularly potent opportunity to reframe your understanding of "failure." Extend your mental model to consider yourself an explorer whenever you are doing or experiencing something new. You're experimenting. You're doing some research. You are pushing through intricacy, unknowns, and uncertainty. You will be more willing to accept that not all of your efforts will result in the outcomes you had hoped for if you approach your life and work through the prism of exploration. It's not a failure. It's all part of what it means to be an explorer. Yes, striving for success should be your main objective. Additionally, it must be learned and found. An explorer's heart and passion are found here. You may change your perspective of failure to one of experimenting and learning, which will help you think more compassionately about yourself.

5. Co-create a "new normal" around caring

When they participate in co-creation, people get a voice and align around goals and interests. We can work with our teams, families, partners, and spouses to co-create a new self-care culture during a period of high stress when everyone is affected. For instance, avoid starting a conversation with a "How are you?" "I'm fine." Rather, together, develop a "new normal" of genuine and compassionate inquiries, such as "How are you feeling today? How are you managing to juggle so many responsibilities? What self-care practices are you following?" These inquiries intrude into people's lives rather than approaching them politely or acting immediately.

As leaders, teams, and families, we can reach a consensus on what it means to take care of ourselves and one another during these trying times. We can agree on the language of care and self-care, on care and self-care frameworks, and on accountability for both self-care and caregiving.

There isn't a single correct response for every person, group, and family. For this reason, truly caring requires co-creating what self-care and care look and feel like. Co-creation respects everyone's experiences and points of view in the new normal. Self-care is both an individual and a team sport. The multifaceted nature of self-care mirrors our lives. A relational dimension exists, a physical dimension exists, both professional and personal dimensions exist, and spiritual dimensions exist. How do we work through those aspects to ensure that we're incorporating self-care and self-compassion into each one? It's important to consider self-compassion and self-care as individual and team sports. We do it for ourselves, one another, and as a group—as families, partners, and teams.

"Take care" is more than just a polite farewell; it's a powerful reminder to prioritize our wellbeing and treat ourselves with kindness, compassion, and respect. By embracing self-care and self-compassion, we can nurture our physical, emotional, and mental health, fostering greater resilience and wellbeing in life's challenges. Whether through mindful self-care practices, self-compassionate self-talk, or seeking support from others, there are countless ways to "take care" and cultivate a life filled with vitality, joy, and inner peace.

CHAPTER NINE

MOVING FORWARD: EMBRACING YOUR POTENTIAL AND ACHIEVING YOUR GOALS

Change is a constant companion on the road of life, guiding us through uncharted territories and presenting opportunities for growth and self-discovery. In the pursuit of success, many of us find ourselves stuck, unable to make meaningful progress toward our goals. We may be filled with aspirations, dreams, and a genuine desire for achievement, but somehow, we must translate these intentions into tangible results. If you're reading this, you may resonate with this struggle, seeking actionable steps to break free from the cycle of stagnation and unlock your true potential. Central to our faith is the belief that God uniquely created each of us and endowed us with gifts, talents, and potential. Embracing your potential begins with recognizing that you are fearfully and wonderfully made with a purpose ordained by God Himself. In life's journey, we often encounter crossroads where we must decide whether to remain stagnant or move forward. Embracing our potential and pursuing our goals is a personal endeavor *and* a spiritual one.

Define Your Vision: The first step towards any objective is to clearly define your goals. Think carefully about your goals and determine what success means to you. Which personal values are the most important to you? Which qualities do you possess? If you match your goals with your abilities and individual values, you'll have the internal drive to see them through. Specify your long-term objectives. Setting relevant goals that fit your career trajectory is more straightforward when your vision is crystal clear. For example: "I want to move up into management so that I can better use my ability to inspire others to work toward a common goal and be in a better position to assist in making decisions that will better align with the needs of our clients." Set SMART Goals: SMART objectives are Time-bound, Relevant, Specific,

Measurable, and Achievable. When defining goals, make sure they are clear and precise, quantifiable to track progress, attainable to sustain motivation, pertinent to your professional ambitions, and time-bound to instill a sense of urgency. For instance, make a SMART objective rather than a too general goal, like "get a promotion." Consider attempting this: "Within the next two years, obtain a leadership position within my department."

Break It Down: Large goals can feel overwhelming and daunting. To prevent this, break down your goals into smaller, actionable steps. Create a roadmap outlining the milestones and actions required to reach your goal. By focusing on these smaller tasks, you can maintain a sense of progress and stay motivated throughout the journey. Remember to keep even your smaller goals SMART. For example, "I will finish one course per month to hone my soft skills in leadership and one course each month to hone my technical skills. Every week, I'll follow up with my supervisor to go over my progress and inquire about any chances to take on extra duties that are pertinent. I'm going to all the forthcoming corporate events so I can connect with the existing leadership internally, etc."

Seek Accountability: Talk about your objectives with a confidant, mentor, or encouraging friend. Making others aware of your objectives fosters a sense of accountability. Frequent check-ins and conversations regarding your development can offer insightful criticism and motivation to help you stay on course. Joining organizations or professional networks might help you meet people who share your interests and who can encourage and support you.

Embrace Continuous Learning: A crucial element of establishing career objectives is determining the abilities and expertise you must get or enhance. Keep up with sector developments and trends to ensure your objectives are still applicable in the changing workplace. Additionally, don't be scared to apply what you're learning to other fields besides your own.

Reflect and Adapt:

1. Review your progress and goals regularly.

2. Think carefully about what is doing well and what needs to be improved.
3. Be willing to modify and revise your goals as you travel toward them if required.

Situations can alter, and fresh chances might present themselves. Accept adaptability and be ready to change course as necessary. Recall that changing your goals is a sign of progress and resilience, not failure.

Honor Milestones: Acknowledge and commemorate your progress throughout the route. Recognizing your accomplishments gives you more self-assurance and inspires you to keep moving forward. Give yourself little treats or time for self-care to help you relax and celebrate your successes. Establishing objectives calls for a calculated plan of action and a dedication to follow through. You can position yourself for success by using this method to achieve each objective. Recall that you can mold your professional path and bring your dreams to fruition. Continue to go forward, maintain your resolve, and remain focused. As we strive to achieve our goals, aligning our aspirations with God's will and purpose is crucial. This involves seeking His guidance through prayer, meditation on Scripture, and discernment of His voice. **Commit to the Lord whatever you do; he will establish your plans**." Proverbs 16:3:"

When we commit our plans to the Lord and seek His direction, He promises to guide and establish our steps. Our goals reflect His purposes for us, leading to greater fulfillment and impact.

As we achieve our goals and experience success in life, we must recognize that all good things come from God. Rather than taking credit for our accomplishments, we are called to acknowledge God's grace and sovereignty humbly.

***"So whether you eat or drink or whatever you do, do it all for the glory of God*.**" 1 Corinthians 10:31:

This verse teaches us to do everything for God's glory. Whether in our achievements or daily activities, we are called to honor and glorify God in all that we do.

CHAPTER TEN

BE BOLD SIS!

In life's journey, we often face obstacles and challenges that threaten our progress and sabotage our dreams. However, the story of Joseph from the Bible serves as a potent reminder that we are more than congruous over sabotage. Through his resilience, faith, and unwavering trust in God, Joseph overcame betrayal, adversity, and injustice to fulfill his destiny and emerge victorious. In this exploration, we'll delve into the story of Joseph and extract timeless lessons on transcending sabotage to achieve our fullest potential.

I am so inspired by the Journey of Joseph. He was destined for greatness from a young age. However, his journey was marked by jealousy, betrayal, and adversity. His brothers, envious of his favor with their father, plotted to kill him but ultimately sold him into slavery. Despite this betrayal, Joseph remained steadfast in his faith and trust in God, ultimately rising to prominence in Egypt as a trusted servant of Potiphar, the captain of the guard.

Trusting in God's Plan: Joseph's story teaches the importance of trusting God's plan, even in adversity and betrayal. Despite the injustice he faced, Joseph remained faithful, believing that God had a purpose for his life. His unwavering trust in God's sovereignty sustained him through the darkest moments of his journey, ultimately leading to his redemption and elevation to a position of power and influence.

Overcoming Betrayal and Adversity: As Joseph's story unfolds, we see him tested and tried in the crucible of betrayal, adversity, and injustice. Potiphar's wife falsely accused Joseph of wrongdoing, and Joseph was thrown into prison, where he languished for years, seemingly forgotten and forsaken. Yet, even in the depths of despair, Joseph clung to his faith and remained steadfast in his commitment to righteousness and integrity.

Resilience in the Face of Adversity: Joseph's resilience in adversity is an inspiring example for us all. Despite his trials and tribulations, Joseph never wavered in his faith or compromised his principles. Instead, he remained steadfast in his commitment to God and maintained his integrity, even when all hope seemed lost. His unwavering resilience ultimately led to his dismissal and exaltation to a position of power second only to Pharaoh himself.

Embracing Forgiveness and Redemption: In a remarkable turn, Joseph's path intersected once again with his brothers, who had come to Egypt seeking food during famine. Though initially tempted to seek revenge, Joseph chose instead to extend forgiveness and reconciliation to his brothers, demonstrating the transformative power of grace and redemption.

The Power of Forgiveness: Joseph's forgiveness towards his brothers is a poignant reminder of the power of grace to heal and restore broken relationships. Rather than harboring bitterness or seeking revenge, Joseph extended mercy and reconciliation, paving the way for healing and restoration within his family. His example challenges us to extend forgiveness to those who have wronged us and embrace grace's transformative power in our lives.

Fulfilling God's Purpose: In the culmination of Joseph's story, we see the fulfillment of God's purpose for his life. Through his trials and triumphs, Joseph was uniquely positioned to save his family and the nation of Egypt from famine, fulfilling the destiny God had ordained for him from the beginning.

Aligning with God's Purpose: Joseph's life exemplifies the importance of aligning our goals and aspirations with God's purpose. Despite his detours and setbacks, Joseph remained faithful to God's calling, trusting in His plan and providence. As a result, he fulfilled a significant role in God's redemptive plan for His people, leaving a legacy of faith, courage, and obedience for generations to come.

The story of Joseph offers timeless lessons on transcending sabotage and achieving our fullest potential. Through his resilience, faith, and unwavering trust in God, Joseph overcame betrayal, adversity, and injustice to fulfill his destiny and emerge victorious. His example challenges us to trust God's plan, remain resilient in adversity, extend forgiveness and grace to others, and align our goals with God's life purpose. As we embrace these lessons and walk in faith, we can overcome sabotage and fulfill the destiny God ordained for us, leaving a legacy of faith, hope, and redemption for generations to come.

CONCLUSION

In conclusion, self-sabotage is a complex and multifaceted behavior that can significantly impact our lives. Throughout this discussion, we have explored the various ways individuals engage in self-sabotaging behaviors, often due to underlying fears, insecurities, or past traumas. Whether it manifests through procrastination, negative self-talk, or self-destructive habits, self-sabotage can hinder our personal growth, success, and overall well-being.

Individuals must recognize and address their self-sabotaging tendencies to break free from destructive patterns and cultivate a healthier relationship with themselves. This process may involve seeking support from therapists, counselors, or trusted loved ones and practicing self-reflection, mindfulness, and self-compassion. By developing a deeper understanding of the root causes of self-sabotage and implementing strategies to overcome these patterns, individuals can take meaningful steps toward unlocking their full potential and living a more fulfilling life.

Remember, you are worthy of love, happiness, and success, and you have the power to break free from self-sabotage and create the life you truly desire. Embrace your strengths, embrace your vulnerabilities, and embrace the journey towards becoming the best version of yourself.

CONNECT WITH DYMEATA

www.dymeatab.com